Space Explorer

THE PLANETS

Patricia Whitehouse

Heinemann Library
Chicago, Illinois

Customer Service 888-454-2279

Visit our website at www.heinemannlibrary.com

Designed by Heinemann Library
Printed in China by South China Printing.

08 07 06 05 04
10 9 8 7 6 5 4 3 2 1

Library of Congress Cataloging-in-Publication Data
Whitehouse, Patricia, 1958-
  The planets / Patricia Whitehouse.
    p. cm. -- (Space explorer)
Includes bibliographical references and index.
ISBN 1-4034-5153-2 (lib. bdg.) -- ISBN 1-4034-5657-7 (pbk.)
1. Planets--Juvenile literature. I. Title. II. Series.
QB602.W48 2005
523.2--dc22
                        2004002439

Acknowledgments
The author and publishers are grateful to the following for permission to reproduce copyright material:

Cover photograph: NASA/Science Photo Library

p. 4 Francisco Diego; p. 5 Joe Lawrence; p. 8 Science Photo Library; p. 9 Science Photo Library; p. 10 Getty Images/Photodisc; p. 12 Getty Images/Photodisc; p. 13 Science Photo Library; p. 14 Freie Universitat Berlin/ESA; p. 15 Corbis (royalty free); p. 16 Getty Images/Photodisc; p. 17 NASA; p. 18 Getty Images/Photodisc; p. 19 Getty Images/Photodisc; p. 20 Hardlines; p. 21 Getty Images/Photodisc; p. 22 NASA/ Science Photo Library; p. 23 Science Photo Library; p. 24 Getty Images/Photodisc; p. 25 Mark Garlick/Science Photo Library; p. 26 Space Telescope Science Institute/NASA; p. 27 Space Telescope Science Institute/NASA; p. 28 Getty Images/Photodisc; p. 29 Science Photo Library

Every effort has been made to contact copyright holders of any material reproduced in this book. Any omissions will be rectified in subsequent printings if notice is given to the publisher.

Special thanks to Geza Gyuk of the Adler Planetarium for his comments in preparation of this book.

Some words are shown in bold, **like this.** You can find out what they mean by looking in the glossary.

Contents

Planets are huge objects in space. They are shaped like a ball. Planets are made of rock, metal, ice, or **gases,** or a combination of these materials. Planets move in a path around a star.

This photo shows the Moon and the planets Venus, Jupiter, and Saturn. These planets along with Mars and Mercury sometimes can be seen from Earth without a telescope.

4

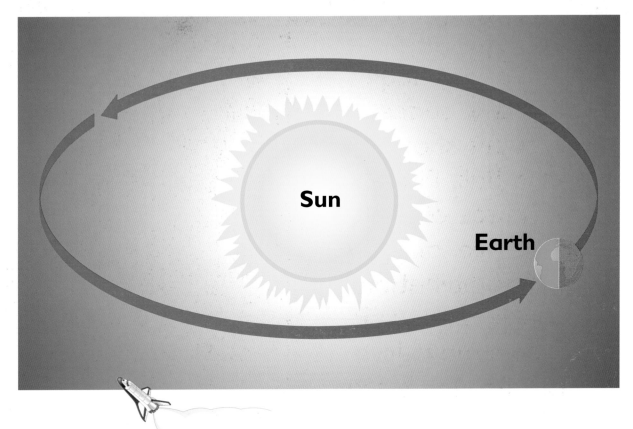

It takes one year for Earth to move once around the Sun.

Earth is a planet. Earth is a ball made mostly of rock and metal. It moves around the star we call the Sun.

The Solar System is made up of the Sun, the planets, and their moons. There are nine planets in the Solar System. Earth is one of the planets.

Sun   Mercury Venus Earth Mars

The planets of the Solar System usually orbit in this order. Earth is the third planet from the Sun.

Each planet in the Solar System has its own path, called an **orbit,** around the Sun. The planets are alike in some ways and different in others.

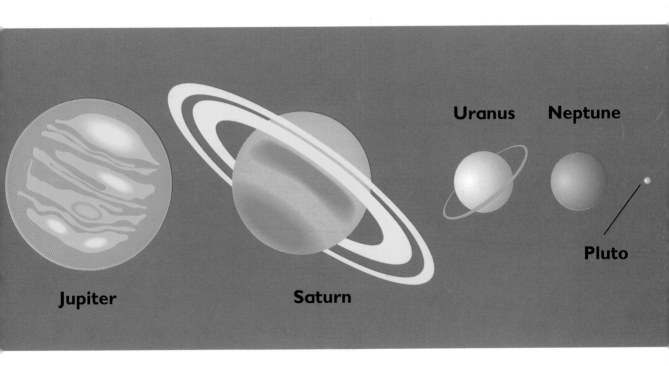

Jupiter

Saturn

Uranus   Neptune

Pluto

Inner Planets and Outer Planets

The four planets closest to the Sun are called the **inner planets.** They are small planets made mostly of rock and metal. They have few or no moons.

Earth is one of the inner planets. The others are Mercury, Venus, and Mars.

The five planets farthest from the Sun are called the **outer planets.** They are Jupiter, Saturn, Uranus, Neptune, and Pluto. The first four of these outer planets are huge and made mostly of gases, so they are called the gas giants.

The four gas giants are Jupiter, Saturn, Uranus, and Neptune.

Mercury

Mercury's **orbit** is closest to the Sun. It is the second-smallest planet in the Solar System. Mercury has no moons.

Space probes have sent photographs of Mercury back to Earth.

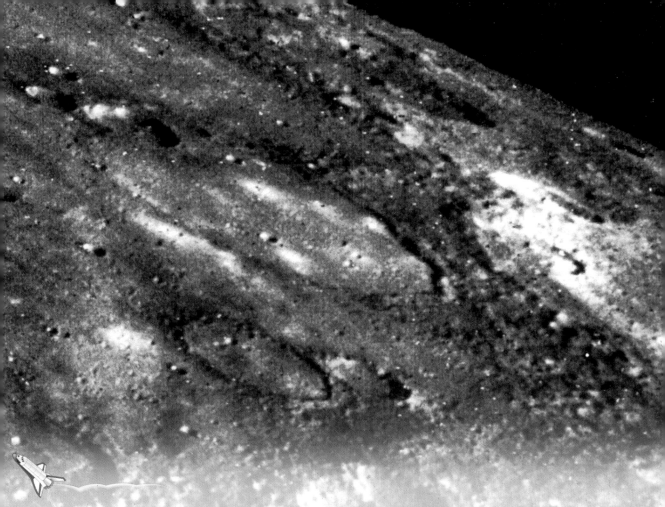

Mercury is covered with holes called craters.

Mercury has no **atmosphere.** The sunny side of Mercury heats up to 860 °F (460 °C). That is hot enough to melt a tin can. The planet's dark side is about 1,080 °F degrees (600 °C degrees) cooler!

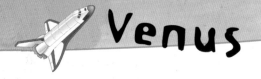

Venus

Venus is the second planet from the Sun. It is sometimes called Earth's twin because both planets are about the same size. Unlike Earth, though, Venus has no moon.

Venus is covered with old volcanoes and lava.

volcano

Venus has a thick **atmosphere** that would be **poisonous** for people to breathe. It is the hottest planet in the Solar System.

Earth

Earth is the third planet from the Sun, and the fifth-biggest. It has only one moon.

Moon

 Earth

This photo shows Earth and the Moon as seen from space.

Earth is probably the only planet in the Solar System that has life on it. It has an **atmosphere** and water. These two things make life possible.

Life probably does not exist on any other planet in the Solar System.

Mars

Mars is the fourth planet from the Sun. It is the seventh-biggest planet. It has two very small potato-shaped moons, called Phobos and Deimos.

Mars is sometimes called the red planet because of its dusty red **surface.** Ice has been found at Mars's north and south poles.

A space probe called Mars Pathfinder landed on Mars and sent pictures like this one back to Earth.

Jupiter is the fifth planet from the Sun. It is the largest planet in the Solar System. It is larger than all the other planets combined! Jupiter has at least 60 moons.

Jupiter is the nearest of the gas giants. A giant storm on its surface is known as the Great Red Spot. The storm has lasted for over 300 years.

Great Red Spot

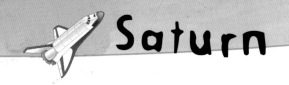

Saturn

The sixth planet from the Sun is Saturn. It is the second-largest planet and is one of the gas giants. It has over 30 moons. One of its moons, called Titan, is bigger than the planet Mercury.

Around Saturn is a band of rings made of rocks and ice. The rings are almost 180,000 miles (300,000 kilometers) wide, but less than $\frac{1}{2}$ mile (1 kilometer) thick.

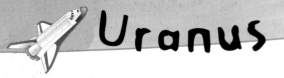

Uranus

Uranus is the seventh planet from the Sun and the third-largest. It has at least 21 moons and a thin, dark band of rings.

This picture of Uranus is made up of many photos put together. That is why its rings cannot be seen.

Uranus is a cold gas giant. It spins on its side, instead of upright like the rest of the planets. Scientists think a huge **asteroid** hit Uranus and knocked it onto its side.

Uranus looks blue-green because of a gas in its atmosphere.

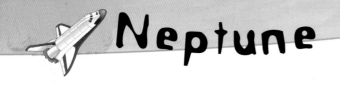

Neptune

Neptune is usually the eighth planet from the Sun. It is about the same size as Uranus. It has at least 11 moons. You need a **telescope** to see Neptune and Uranus from Earth.

Neptune is made mostly of **gases** and ice and has faint rings like Uranus. Storms sometimes appear as dark spots on its surface.

Great Dark Spot

One storm, called the Great Dark Spot, was as big as Earth.

Pluto

Pluto is usually the ninth planet from the Sun. Part of its **orbit** is inside Neptune's, so sometimes it is the eighth planet from the Sun.

Pluto, the smallest planet in the Solar System, has a moon called Charon.

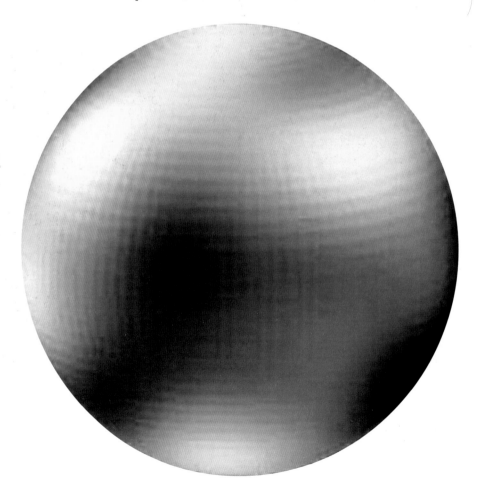

Unlike the other **outer planets,** Pluto is made of a mixture of ice and rock. Scientists know little about Pluto because it is so far from Earth.

Charon

Pluto

Pluto is about twice the size of its moon, Charon.

Other Planets

Astronomers have found other objects at the edges of the Solar System. But these objects are too small to be called planets.

Astronomers use **telescopes in space** to help them look for other planets.

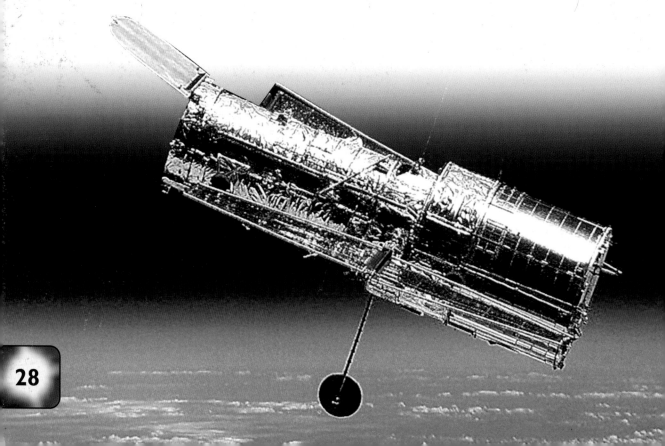

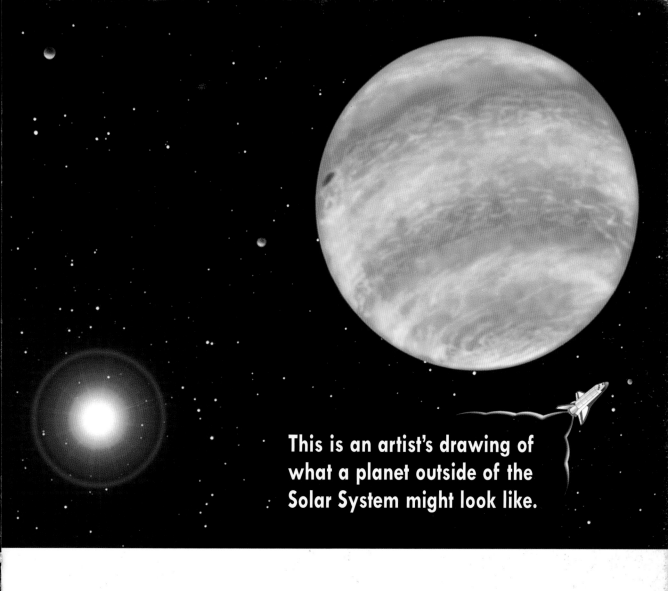

This is an artist's drawing of what a planet outside of the Solar System might look like.

Using new telescopes, astronomers have found over 100 planets outside the Solar System. Could there be life on these planets? Someday, astronomers may find out.

Amazing Planet Facts

- The temperature on Venus can reach 878 °F (470 °C), which is hot enough to melt lead.

- Winds on Neptune can reach 600 miles (1,000 kilometers) per hour.

- Four of Jupiter's moons can be seen from Earth using binoculars.

- Some scientists think that there are diamonds in the center of Uranus.

Glossary

asteroid large rocky objects that orbit the Sun

astronomers scientists who study space

atmosphere layer of gases around a planet

gas airlike material that is not solid or liquid

inner planets four planets closest to the Sun

orbit the path one object makes around another

outer planets the five planets farthest from the Sun

poisonous harmful

space probe a spacecraft that sends information back to Earth about space

surface the top or outside of an object

telescope an instrument used to make faraway objects look bigger

More Books to Read

Whitehouse, Patricia. *Sun (Space Explorer)*. Chicago: Heinemann Library, 2004.

Whitehouse Patricia. *The Earth (Space Explorer)*. Chicago: Heinemann Library, 2004.

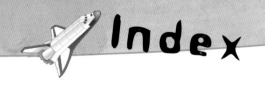

Index